# EX LIBRIS

Margaret Beard
Jan 79

LET'S LOOK AT

# Design

# LET'S LOOK AT

# Design

*by*

## C. G. Tomrley

*Illustrated by*

## Geoffrey Trenaman

FREDERICK MULLER

First published in Great Britain in 1969 by
Frederick Muller Limited, 110 Fleet Street, London, E.C.4

Copyright © 1969 by C. G. Tomrley

*Phototypeset by BAS Printers Limited, Wallop, Hampshire*
*Printed by Fleming & Humphreys (Baylis) Ltd, Leicester*
*Bound by Wm. Brendon & Son Ltd, Tiptree*

SBN: 584 63415 3

LET'S LOOK AT

# Design

Everything is designed. Birds and animals are designed, so
are vegetables, flowers and fruit. Here Nature, not Man, is
the designer. Design by human beings of what they use and
enjoy cannot help following the same lines as design by
Nature.

A bird is a beautifully designed creature. To fly it must be
very light but have power. A bird's bones are accordingly
full of air spaces and its feathers, themselves light, are
arranged so that those on the body streamline it, and those on
the wings can fan it along. The plumage and voice of a bird
are designed to attract other birds of the opposite sex and like
kind. Each summer, when a bird's plumage has become
shabby through the hard work of rearing nestlings, a new set
of feathers replaces the old in time to withstand weather or
the long journeys undertaken by migrants. If you watch birds
seeking their food, you will see that their problem is expressed

by the shape of the head and position of the eyes—the bird is able to spot tit-bits on the ground while still watching for enemies approaching from above. This is to say nothing of the remarkable direction finding system built into migrant birds.

These considerations and others, which might be called the 'specification', added together make a plan for the design of a bird. For an object made by Man the specification embodies similar considerations, chiefly:

What the object has to do, or its *function*
How long it must last, or its *durability*
How attractive it must be, or its *appearance*.

A bird of the air must be able to fly, to live on what it can easily find and be furnished with a lightweight renewable waterproof cover. A washing machine must wash clothes efficiently and safely and its motor must not break down. Your handkerchief must be right in size and colour, must stand boiling, be absorbent and not be scratchy and stiff. If something does its job well it earns the description 'functional'.

If a thing lasts well it is said to be 'durable'. Barring accidents birds and animals have the durability—life span— suited to their rate of reproduction. Elephants have fewer young than rabbits. Their design for durability must also suit their normal environment and its hazards. If a man-made article does not last well it becomes a poor bargain. A designer must design a product so that it fulfils the reasonable expectations of its owner, and it fails to do this if a part collapses when it is fairly new, or if holes appear quickly, or if paint chips off easily, or it seems carelessly made and constantly needs repair.

The appearance of an object should be attractive to those whom it is intended to please. In the animal kingdom attractiveness has the straightforward purpose of perpetuating the species. The designer of a man-made object has to know broadly the 'species'—or the type—of human being he is designing for, and what will seem attractive to them. They may be known as 'the market'. A designer must study his market and give it the best design he believes it will accept. People are not always able to appreciate good design. They are carried away by superficialities.

The word design covers all three parts of the specification: function, durability and appearance. As designers are the representatives of the consumers in the factories, they have to look after all three and so designing involves all three. Nevertheless, equal weight and consideration cannot be given to all three. Before a design is begun, it must be decided which one is the most important.

Our new electric cooker

1. MUSTS.
   must'nt be wider than 1'9, and bet
   " stick out more than 2' not less
                                  max
   must be same height as my working
      tops, 3 ft
   Note what if none 3ft, higher or lower?
   must have 4 hotplates, 3 at least
      on simmerstats
   must have some way of warming
      plates and dishes (but see 3 below)
   must allow easy mopping of space
      under hotplates

2 DESIRABLE
   as much as poss. of oven take-out-
      able for cleaning? top as well
   glass inner oven door
   grill under hob not above
   keep - food - warm drawer
   adjustment for uneven floor
   controls away from steaming pans
   oven timer - yes if poss
   a dual hotplate if poss (for
      those small pans)

Clothes bought in Carnaby Street, London, or in boutiques for young people, have the emphasis on appearance. When appearance is almost all-important it is called 'fashion'. The essence of fashion is short-lived emphatic design. One does not expect boutique clothes to be built to last. They would then be too costly and the purchaser would not have the money to buy new as soon as the fashion changed.

On the other hand a carpet is, of its nature, an expensive item. Consequently people expect them to last and look well for years. A balding carpet is a horrible sight, so it is unthinkable to manufacture them really cheaply. Attractive surface design makes no difference if the surface wears off. As the surface design must last with the carpet, it must not be too fashionable to begin with or it will quickly look out of date. Conversely, if you see a fashionable-looking carpet, it is likely to be of low quality. Thus durability is the most important of our three considerations here, and after that, appearance; the colour, pattern and texture. The function is simple and belongs to the very idea of a carpet, which is to make the floor feel softer and warmer. Additionally it must lie flat without stretching yet not be so stiff that it cannot be rolled and handled.

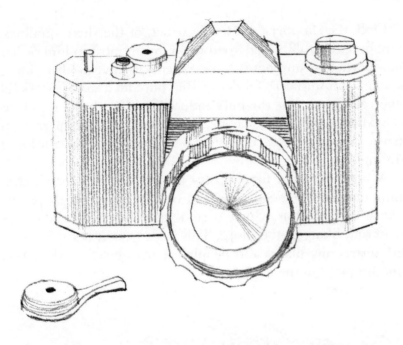

A camera is no use unless all its parts work together to take good pictures. So function, as with most objects with moving parts, is of primary importance. Durability comes next. It is no use if little bits of a camera drop off while its owner is on holiday. Its good appearance rests on making the owner feel proud to own it because it looks a good quality article. An expensive article which looks cheap and uninteresting does not make commercial sense.

You will find that these three considerations, perhaps under other names, underlie all human designing. But, as we have seen, they may be differently balanced.

Only the shopper can decide which of the three qualities, function, durability and good looks, mean most to him or her in a particular purchase. Nature seems to have a self-righting system—an unsuccessful design dies out and a more successful one carries on. But the only industrial self-righting system is the knowledge and clear-headedness of the shopper. It is never too soon to learn to shop well and it can save a lot of disappointment.

A human design for industry always depends for its continuation on sales. Sales depend on whether enough people like it and trust it. Good design must therefore encourage trust and liking in the shops. This is important because shops are distracting places and people are not always at their best and brightest in them.

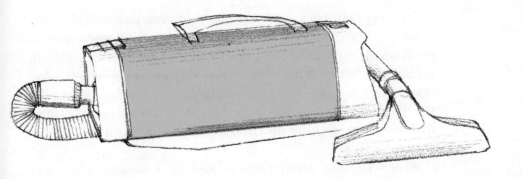

When people shop they must decide—or better, have decided—which of our three qualities matters most in what they are about to buy. Two of them, function and durability, encourage trust; the other, good looks, encourages liking. If what is on offer has all these advantages in the right order of importance it is likely to be a good buy. The shopper has only to compare its price with others and see if it is worth the money to be spent.

Sometimes it is difficult to decide whether a complicated piece of machinery like a vacuum cleaner or a scooter can be trusted. Here the experiences of other shoppers and the manufacturer's reputation may help.

In most countries, and especially in America and Britain, there are organisations which test and report upon consumer equipment, especially the expensive, and what is considered potentially dangerous. These reports, intended chiefly for members, may, nevertheless, be studied in libraries. Naturally the date of the reports must be taken into account since manufacturers frequently eliminate faults brought to light in these analyses.

Much modern equipment is sold in a casing. The consumer's only contact with the working parts is by means of knobs and switches. The casing both protects the works and captivates the consumer by its up-to-date look. A casing is easier and cheaper for the manufacturer to change than the works inside, and a washing machine stripped of its glamorous white box would be rather a daunting object to many mothers of families.

WHICH report on Children's Bicycles 8/68
All of 23 tested needed adjustment when new
Two sizes tested, for 3-6's, (13) + over 7's (10)
All U.K. made + for boys or girls
Frame size is the distance bet. top of
saddle tube to centre of bottom bracket
(where pedals pinned in) Child's
inside leg meas. shd = top of saddle to
ground
See that bike has generous adjustment for growth.
Weight small, around 20 lb, larger 22-27
Tyres few solid (hard), 7 balloon (vulnerable)
rest inflatable ordinary (See that
bike sold with pump if nec.)
Extras One folds in ½. Some had tools
Safety You must check in shop for stiff-
ness, looseness, wobbles, tightness.
Brakes Best on both wheels. Over 3" too much
bet. handlebars + brake grips
Pedal clearance for cornering - watch it
Sharp edges watch them
Durability rating - given as result of lab tests
Best buy Cost £17.17.0

These casings of course tend to obscure the merits or demerits of what is inside. The fact that the lovely new case of this year's model conceals last year's works may not be a bad thing. It depends how good the engineering design was in the first place. At least the shopper buys a well-tried mechanism.

The customer's only protection against undue influence by glamour is a very clear picture, built up at home or with friends, of what the machine—perhaps this washing machine —really must do: the size it must not exceed, the real need for complete automation, its cost to run, how long it must last to be worth its price, and so on. Knowing how to ask the right questions is nine-tenths of being a good shopper.

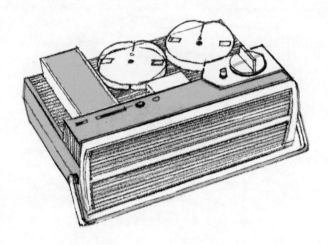

You may be asking for a present of a tape-recorder or
record player. Here, if you are wise, you will not ask for the
one which glows most with colour, chromium plating and
gadgets. You are, in fact, buying a scientifically-designed
instrument. The research put into the design of top quality
sound recorders and reproducers has helped the instruments
which give young people so much pleasure. But makers often
pay these young people the backhanded compliment of
supposing that they will be caught by a fashionable, rather
brash exterior treatment. The primary need is for an item of
sound, stout construction and reasonable weight for port-
ability.

A brash exterior treatment? Brash means eye-catching and the eye caught is one that is attracted to something showy. The person behind the eye may, nevertheless, be caught with a poor bargain.

The words connected with appearance are:

    style;
    fashion;
    styling.

First, style. Everyone had heard of 'period styles'. To hear some people talk one would think that something like car-spotter's-eye was all that a student of period styles needed. They are however highly significant expressions of the moods and tastes of people long dead. It is nevertheless true that experts can recognise antique objects by certain features which provide the clues to those with profound knowledge. They can date a pot or vase or figurine by tell-tale features of shaping, materials and decoration much as one recognises a friend at a distance, or know whose writing is on the envelope you pick up from the mat.

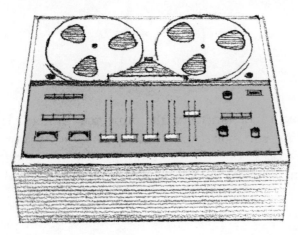

In all cases, such recognition takes place through the 'style' of the person or object. Very simply, style is a quality of total appearance which encourages recognition. To recognise the purpose for which an object was made may demand a knowledge of the habits of the time. Take a lidded silver pot. A well-informed expert will say 'This is a chocolate pot, not a coffee pot, as it has a little hole in the lid through which a sort of swizzle stick was put to ensure that the lumps of chocolate were melted before they were allowed to clog the spout'. Style tells you how to place and date an object and where to look for other details such as its function.

Will people be able to recognise and date present-day things in one hundred years' time? Certainly. We can already

date furniture designed in the nineteen thirties. It has a wholly different look from that fashionable in the middle nineteen sixties. But the most dating features about it are certain immediately noticeable design tricks known as 'design clichés'.

Fashionable words and phrases are often called 'clichés'. Some are good and telling, a short way of saying much, like the two words 'with it'. Others are boring and silly. The most dating features of a design are very like these word clichés. A few years—or months—later they seem very odd. Just after the Second World War most furniture seemed to have splayed tapering legs like a milking stool. Such legs have obvious disadvantages, one being that they trip up people, another being that it is very difficult to fix into a finely tapering leg the stiffening bars which prevent chair or table legs from loosening. But despite this, designers everywhere seemed to feel the need for this same cliché at the same time. It is not always easy to distinguish between a design cliché and a major stylistic feature. Which applies, for example, to the typical early eighteenth-century chair leg known as a 'cabriole leg'? (see page 56). Certainly this notable piece of construction with its delicately carved 'claw and ball' foot, seems, however fashionable, to merit respect.

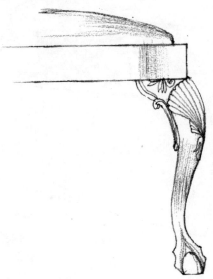

People tend to accept the stylistic features which the best designers of the time feel to be right. If there is scope in them for invention and refinement of design and for first-class workmanship, stylistic features become more than the equivalent of cheap catch phrases.

At the seaside you may have watched the movement of water. Beyond the beach, the incoming tide causes quite large bodies of water to come shorewards. But if there is a breeze, the surface of the water will be stirred by choppy wavelets. Something of the same sort can be seen in the evolution of design. There is a long-term trend, such as a gradual movement from decorated architecture or furniture towards the plain and severe. But if one focuses upon detail, one finds that fashion causes endless short-term variations. At the time, the new ones were delightful, the ones on the way out, boring. This is the essence of fashion.

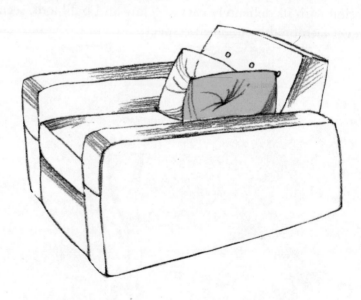

Now we have a new problem, the word for which is 'styling'. Anything can be 'styled' from your newspaper to your car, but the word is usually applied to the changes given by manufacturers of expensive, durable goods to the easily-modified exterior which conceals the much less easily modified engineering within. The research and development costs of re-engineered and re-tooled models are so high that something has to be done to ensure continued sales during the years when no fundamental redesign is offered. Many people like to give the impression that they can afford a 'new' model whenever one appears, as a status symbol. We must surely be a little clearheaded about such matters, and at least recognise our true motives, paying for them if we must.

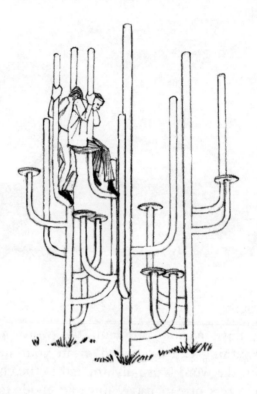

Style, fashion, styling and clichés are the chief special words used for appearance in industrially-made goods.

These words are, however, not much use to a designer and they do not form part of his designer's vocabulary. A designer is thinking about and using the basic ingredients of design.

These are:

*Form*  Shape, modelling. Form is three-dimensional.

*Line*  The element in a design which tows the eye in a particular direction. The eye is towed along a building if features such as windows or mouldings make horizontal lines, and up and down a building if it has emphatic verticals in columns or a stack of staircase windows. Line is two-dimensional.

*Colour*  A splendid tool for a designer but especially important with textiles, carpets, wallpapers and the like, whose flat surface is what is chiefly seen and whose play of colour is their chief selling feature.

*Pattern*  This supplies the element of rhythm. We can talk about the pattern of a tune or of a poem and of pattern on a curtain or dress. Rhythm always has repetition of some sort. Without that it is not rhythm. A page of type has a tiny little rhythm making it soothing and easy to read. A curtaining intended for large halls will have a much larger rhythm of design. Pattern is usually two-dimensional.

*Texture*  This arises from materials and finishes. A Persian cat's fur is different from that of a Siamese. Knitting has a special texture of its own which can be both seen and felt. A car is perfectly smooth, shiny and cold. An antique table is satiny rather than shiny and warmer.

You can become a connoisseur (knower) of all these things without becoming a designer. A designer, however, learns about them as part of his special training.

Most designers are trained in schools of art. Others, of course, if you extend the word designer as far as it will go, are trained in schools of architecture and engineering. Schools of art train designers and award diplomas in the following kinds of industrial design:

*Three-dimensional*
    Design for engineered products, plant and equipment
      (mostly of metal or plastics)
    Furniture
    Pottery and Glass
    Silverware and jewellery, cutlery and hand-tools
    Interior design.

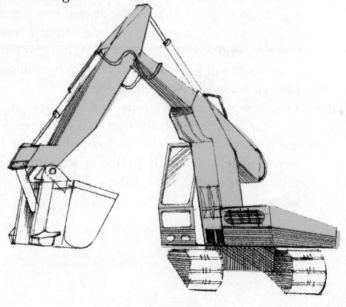

*Two-dimensional*
   Textiles, woven and printed
   Floor coverings, woven and printed
   Flexible plastic sheeting
   Rigid plastic sheeting
   Wallpaper
   Machine embroidery.

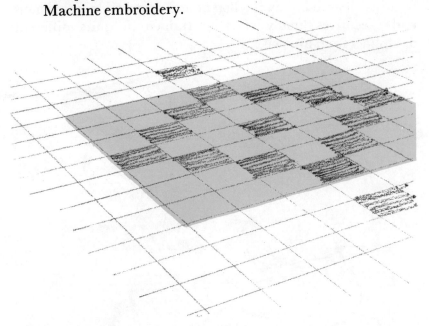

The designers in three-dimensions (except for interiors) are for the most part, and with a few notable exceptions, men. In the two-dimensional fields women predominate.

There is also a very vigorous sphere of activity known as 'graphic design'. This includes the design of books and all uses of the printed word, advertising and packaging.

The training of a designer takes five to seven years and nowadays five 'O' levels at least are required for a qualifying course. Without a good, well-disciplined brain, the modern designer is severely handicapped. This is because, (*a*) he is likely to have to do advanced calculation, (*b*) he has to come to intelligent decisions about his proposals, based on considerable investigation, technical and social, (*c*) he has to put over his ideas to highly intelligent and responsible technicians and executives, many of them trained in quite different disciplines from his own.

All this should suggest that designing is very far from just dreaming up ideas. It refers to real brainwork. In addition, the designer has to have that mysterious ability often called 'creative'. He must also be able to do whatever types of drawing are current in his factory so that colleagues of all grades will understand what his proposals are. And, very important, he must know enough about production processes to be very sure that he is not proposing something impossible or expensive to make.

The way a design for a product comes into being depends on which of our three considerations, function, durability and appearance, is to be foremost. Of the first two, the ones that encourage trust, function is the one most pressing upon the designer or design team. Durability comes about rather through the combined body of knowledge in the works. It is hard, without built-up experience, to foresee what will go wrong with a product in use.

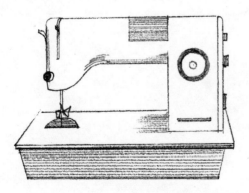

But function these days may well have to be re-thought for every new product. Some are machines used to make other products; here it is imperative to study newly-invented methods—for example, the many uses of electronics and of lasers—and all the designers concerned, whether engineers or others, will have to re-examine function all the time. Consumer products such as furniture need re-examination in the light of changing living habits and what people can afford to spend; durable household equipment must progress towards greater convenience in use, smaller size, reduced weight, reduced price (often achieved through better production methods) and greater safety in use.

The so-called craft-based products—pottery, glass, silverware—traditionally hand-made, are now largely made by machine, and the designer's problem is to retain some of the enchanting quality of the best traditional ware, while gaining the advantage of low price and ready availability. In two-dimensional design fashion is important. Textiles, wallpapers and plastic surfaces can be easy and cheap to renew. They are the main carriers of colour and pattern in the home and people need change here rather as they discard and renew their clothes.

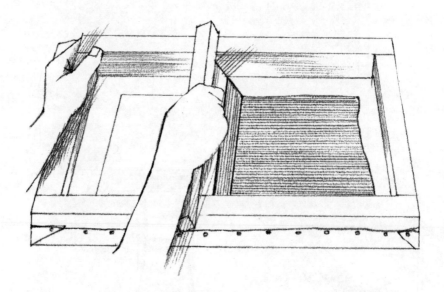

So you may allow yourselves to visualise the textile designers either working on large drawing boards with pencil, brush and colour, or doing experimental photography as a preliminary to screen printing or actually making their own screens and printing their own cloth, to gain effects that they hope can be obtained in industry when the design is sold. Many two-dimensional designs are manufactured from a hand-made prototype looking very like what finally comes on to the market.

Prototypes are also nearly always made for three-dimensional products, but for the sake of cheapness this is the final stage of the design. Several models or 'mock-ups' in wood, plaster or even paper precede it, and the designer's preliminary drawings are often the kind from which a small or full-scale model can be made, but not yet the drawings needed for a final prototype in actual production materials.

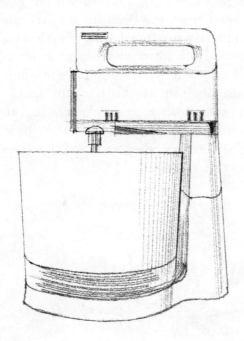

At model stage weaknesses in design can be spotted. It is the first time a designer has seen all round his design. However careful he is, a technical drawing may not warn him of an ugly view along one line of sight. He can easily and cheaply alter it at that stage. A model, too, is an easy thing for all concerned, right up to the Board of Directors, to discuss.

Designers of three-dimensional objects must therefore be not only draughtsmen in every sense, but sculptors as well.

Most of this refers to the efforts of art-school-trained designers to design mass- or quantity-produced goods. There are still many hand processes used in industry and the first ever of many quantity-produced things such as a silver or stainless steel spoon, a bathroom basin or a set of drinking glasses may well be made by traditional workshop methods. Designers are usually taught the relevant hand processes. They work on a potter's wheel or do clay casting, they do fine hand-loom weaving, they print textiles, they beat up silver shapes on special formers, they cut and hammer stainless steel, they may even blow or mould glass.

Their future will probably, however, be either as members of works design teams, or design teams run by consultants. They will have to learn to think in terms of the reproduction of their designs in thousands.

About thirty years ago a pioneer of the modern movement in design, the architect Serge Chermayeff, said 'Mass production is a heaven-sent opportunity for multiplying good design'. He was right, but the same applies to bad design though it is most certainly not heaven-sent.

Numbers of people exist with a talent for design. No one knows where talent comes from and we might as well look on it as a present from heaven. If you are one of the lucky ones with a strong talent, it is just as well that you should get yourself trained in order to use it fully and well. On the way you will learn to be a craftsman, a satisfying activity.

The satisfaction of the designer-craftsman with his own small business extends to his customers and a better living may be made by fine craftsmen now than ever before. This has been true in Scandinavia for many years; there the traditions of fine craftsmanship have never flagged and after the Second World War Swedish and Danish products enjoyed world-wide appreciation, and are indeed the aristocrats of their kind. The Swedes, Danes and Finns excel at pottery, glass, lighting fittings, silverware, pewterware, furniture and textiles, a very fine achievement.

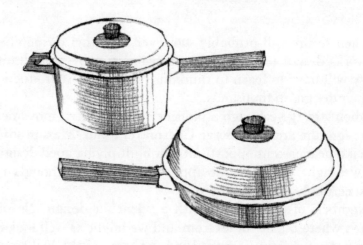

In industrialised countries hand-work is not absent from the factories, though the creative aspects of craftsmanship are not present. Some furniture is hand-finished, although the process is so standardised that one can detect no difference between one sideboard and another. In the motor industry elaborate and highly finished mock-ups are made by specially trained craftsmen, capable of working alongside designers.

The consumer does not feel the benefit of this kind of hand work. Whereas two industrially produced teacups will be much more alike than two prize budgerigars, two hand-made chairs may differ from one another rather as two budgies do. They have personality. This is the essential thing which distinguishes work from the hand of a single craftsman from factory products, and it is probably why an increasing number of people like to have a few hand-made treasures about them, and why they haunt the junk-shops where many nice things may still be cheaply bought.

Hand-made objects of utility tend to be pleasant to handle and use. In industry where products are in the first stages designed on paper and may be considerably developed before anything is made which a person could experimentally handle, it has become necessary to remind designers about the right of the user to be comfortable with what he uses. A special science, called in Britain 'ergonomics' and the United States 'human engineering', has been developed to study the needs and habits of men, women and children in relation to the things they use. These, as it were, impose their will upon us and if badly designed frustrate us. Ergonomic studies among designers and design engineers should help to eliminate tiredness, soreness and irritation arising from awkward design.

Special attention has been devoted to seating, not so much domestic chairs, but first, pilot's and aircrew seating, then industrial seating, and more recently office, theatre and school seating. The needs of people who perform some task seated for a long time cannot be decided offhand. The study of ergonomics is spreading back among the things which in the old days the craftsmen did exactly right—for example, the handles of tools.

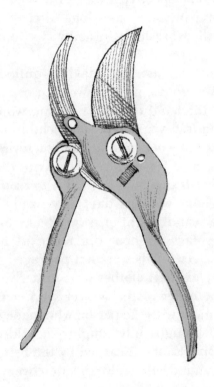

The study of ergonomics brings home to us the extra-ordinary feats the same old human body is now expected to perform. The ultimate up to the present is existence in spacecraft. It helps to put the present rapid pace of discovery and invention into perspective if we realise the following:

Before 1800 and in some cases long after, everything was made in small workshops, usually by one individual craftsman.

Any machinery in use for making quite complicated wooden or metal goods, pots, or woollen or cotton textiles, was driven by the hand or foot of a man, woman or child. Just over a hundred years ago, small children as young as four or five went to work in mines and factories. It was rare for such children to learn to read or write then or at any time in their life. If they had been able to read, and willing after their ten hour working day, they would have had to do it by rush or candle light or if very lucky by oil lamp.

Shops with displays of goods did not exist until about a hundred years ago. Foods were not packaged; ready-made clothing hardly existed; clothes were either made at home or made to the order of the wearer who could meet and discuss the garment with the person who made it.

Many people, though fully employed, seldom had new clothes, but wore clothes discarded by the better-off. In the early nineteen hundreds children often went barefoot in the industrial north.

Before 1914 plastics were hardly known.

Nylon stockings were new and rare in 1940 and people were hoarding silk stockings well into the Second World War.

The first 'man-made-fibres', then called artificial silk and later rayon, only developed into acceptable textiles between the wars, and have since been replaced by newer fibres such as terylene and nylon.

There has been little change in the fine linen cloths available in Europe, Asia and Africa since the Egyptians made them from flax some 2,000 years ago. These and fine cottons have simply been supplanted, and this in about thirty years.

*Lathe, 1850-1900*

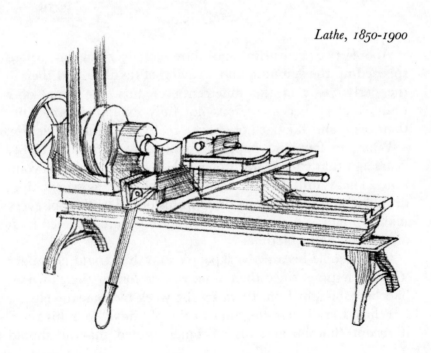

About two centuries ago, however, certain inventions speeded up the spinning and weaving of textiles. And then in the early years of the nineteenth century the fruits of a number of earlier inventions not fully exploited came into their own, and the pace of change really began to accelerate.

What, in fact, did happen about a hundred and eighty years ago that caused this upheaval? The Industrial Revolution. These dull words cover one of the most exciting, dramatic and momentous times in history. The lives of every man, woman and child in western society were changed by it and within half a lifetime.

Craftspeople became workpeople and they could no longer 'take their time' since their time was no longer their own; it had been bought from them by the week by someone else.

When a craftsman-designer in the old days 'took his time' it meant that he and his customer agreed that he should produce a beautiful object no matter how long it took. The craftsman was encouraged to dwell on his design, elaborate it, refine it, invent decoration, perhaps using other materials. Gold, ivory, jewels, fine porcelain, could be ordered by the patron prepared to pay for them. Decoration was often in one of the more valuable materials which needed special tools to work them. The craftsman usually made the tools, as he could not order them from a catalogue. Such a fine craftsman made a living but he worked exceedingly long hours and was certainly not among the leisured classes. These were his patrons, his customers.

Quite suddenly the whole climate of making, buying and selling changed and it changed because steam was applied to driving not only railway engines and steamships but machines used to make things.

A steam-driven machine, unlike a hand-propelled one, was not something you could have in your home. Steam, to be worth while, had to be produced where-there were numbers of machines and gangs of workpeople. These were the first factories and in them a worker looked after a single process instead of the whole workpiece as before. Naturally this new system resulted in faster production and cheaper goods, the fortunes made by the factory owners brought a new class of rich person, and the flow of goods caused the development of shops with displays and stocks, smaller editions of the ones we know.

The old-style designer-craftsman did not become the designer for the new factories. The designer for factory-produced goods in the nineteenth century was at first someone who had flair and could read. He looked up the illustrated books on design, of which there were many, full of engravings, not photographs, of course, and he copied what was in them, making adaptations to suit machine production. The more cheaply goods had to be made, the more uneducated 'the market' (the new purchasers who had seldom had new things of their own), the more debased designs became.

Even those newly enriched, who could have afforded elegant possessions, had had insufficient education or opportunity to enrich their minds. Travel, one of the most educative of pursuits, was not open to the man who was making his money by dint of the heavy daily grind of running the works. By the time he had amassed a fortune he had still had no opportunity to develop his taste, study the best in art and literature, read deeply and widely or learn to recognise quality and style.

The result was design by the uneducated for the uneducated, and an upsurge of ugly and expensive houses and goods to put in them. No one was to blame.

Not unnaturally protesting voices were raised, not just among architects, then the only fully trained professional designers, but from a band of dedicated men, painters and potential designers, who came to be known as the Pre-Raphaelites.

*William Morris chair*

Several of them, and foremost William Morris, protested on social rather than aesthetic grounds. For many years Morris was a heated opponent of industry and especially of the features in the new industrial methods which deprived workers of a creative interest in their work, and deprived the rest of society of the results of this creative interest.

Morris and his friends attempted to practise what they preached and set up workshops and a retail shop. But the climate of the time was not in their favour, they did not have a commercial success and now the products of their workshops and printing press are only seen in museums.

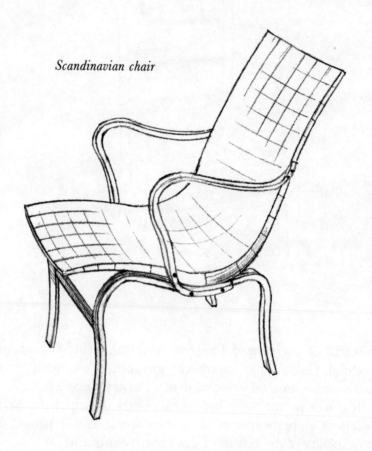

*Scandinavian chair*

But Morris's views left their mark, They were studied in Germany and Scandinavia. He had a direct influence on the training of generations of British designers who might otherwise just have learned to copy designs of less and less merit.

Now, throughout Britain, Europe and America trained industrial designers are available and are used. But will the design profession be able to keep pace with the enormous speed of technological development?

Provided that industrial designers have brains and are in sympathy with technology—rather as many young boys seem to be born in sympathy with motor-cycles—there is no reason why the design profession should not be in the forefront of new ideas. But it is now clear why the training of a qualified designer will take five years, and may take six or seven.

The encouragement of creativity, or the sparking off of ideas, is only a part of it. Creativity can be applied to science, engineering and mathematics as easily as to art and design. Here you have a profession involved with all of these.

It is only recently that anyone has thought of separating them. Leonardo da Vinci was a brilliant mathematician and inventor as well as one of the greatest painters the world has seen. His drawings of inventions can be studied now in a museum in Italy.

The history of design offers a good view of the emergence of new ideas provided that one approaches from the right direction and studies evolution as it happened.

Let us think, for example, about the chair.

We must start before there were any. Primitive men and women lived on the floor and did not think of cooking, eating, making tools or weaving except in a squatting attitude.

Among such people a stool becomes the equivalent of a throne. With primitive tools they could not do much jointing and the easiest way of making a stool, time being no object, was to chop it and hollow it from a larger piece of wood.

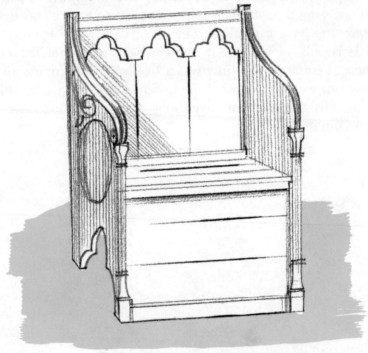

*Early oak chair, thirteenth century*

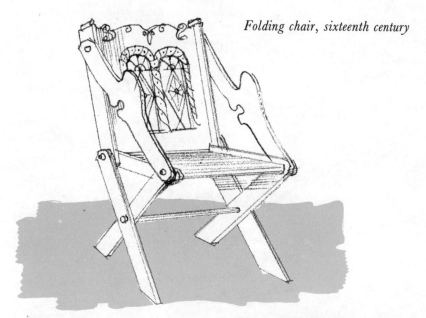

*Folding chair, sixteenth century*

Designs had to be suited to the tools available. This has always been true. In Europe tools were comparatively rudimentary up to the thirteenth century. The carving in a Gothic cathedral expresses the action of his tools in the hands of a wood- or stone-carver, and in the same way the crude wooden furniture of the time looked as if it had been made by the same man as the church font, or his neighbour.

Visualise one man carving the *miserere* seats and the other the font, quite without drawings, designing as they went along; similar men doing a similar job, and both designers.

If one of them had turned to domestic seating for the manor house, it would have been the woodworker. Oak, a hard wood, was usual. Though there were stools, chairs were a rarity up to 1500 in England.

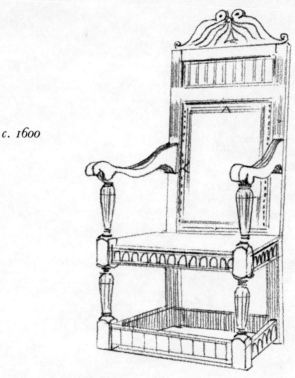

*c. 1600*

The throne is the ancestor of the armchair and when after 1500 these came in, they were a status symbol. On big chairs with towering backs and curling arms sat kings and overlords, very stiffly upright, knees together, looking every inch a dignitary.

We may be sure that great effort went into the development of armchairs, stimulated by high-level pressures from the great ones who wanted their chairs to be the best ever. So eventually canvas or carpet were used to sit on and then finer materials padded with sheeps wool. Then the back and arms were padded as well and we have the beginnings of chairs designed for comfort. Previously design had been dictated by the use of one material, hardwood, and one craftsman with his traditional kit of woodworking tools. Once the client asked for padding, it opened the way for the use of fine woven or embroidered cloth, in glowing colours.

But we still have about three centuries to go before comfort —that is, one of the prime functions of a chair—was intended. This is surprising in that a multitude of skills became available, and by the end of the seventeenth century almost anything designed could have been made.

In the seventeenth century oak was superseded for grand chairs by walnut, a finer-grained wood well suited to elaborate carving and taking a fine polish. A new style of chair came over from Holland with the returning Charles II; it was tall and narrow and made of walnut with carving concentrated in two places, behind the sitter's head and behind his calves. The carving was scroll-like and pierced. Behind the sitter's back, as a concession to comfort, was a small panel of cane work or thin padding which was repeated in the seat. The legs were carved, often with the 'barley-sugar twist'. These chairs were better to look at than to sit on. Since they were made in sets, they were not always occupied, and did well to look beautiful.

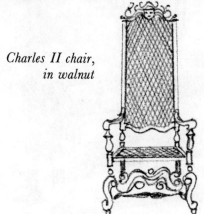

*Charles II chair,*
*in walnut*

During the reign of Queen Anne, 1702–1714, a homely style of interior design and furniture became the admiration of Europe. Was it feminine influence or coincidence that at the time of this Queen smooth, well-upholstered chairs were made in sets so that everyone could be seated? And that they were so often covered in needlework, each chair slightly different?

The chair continued its progress towards comfort and in Queen Anne's reign the first real easy chairs were made, fully upholstered and having a high back curving round the sitter like a padded wall, terminating at the sides in wings—hence the 'wing chair' of the present day. Matching footstools were provided. But, probably because of their stiff clothing, the sitters still sat upright.

*Queen Anne chair*

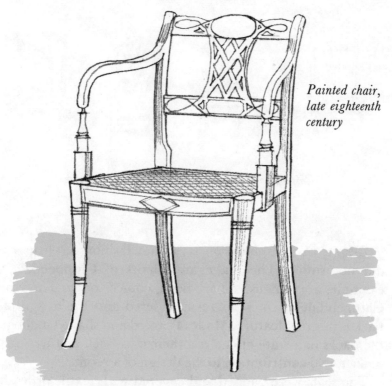

*Painted chair,
late eighteenth
century*

In the eighteenth century great furniture craftsmen
flourished, and several of these were great designers. However,
because of the extensive European travel fashionable among
their distinguished clients, these designers often had to design
to fit a prescribed foreign taste which became all the rage in
interior design, and change their style of design as the fashion
changed. A client's wishes were often interpreted to the
craftsman by an interior architect, who acted as designer-in-
chief.

*Chippendale, Adam, Hepplewhite and Sheraton*

Despite the emphasis on style and fashion, craftsmanship did not suffer. The mahogany chairs of Chippendale, for example, are famous and are being copied today. The typical Chippendale chair is broad-shouldered and the design of its back is its great feature. Made of carved and shaped mahogany the backs of a suite of chairs—their most seen feature—could make a real contribution to the design of a room.

The seats were padded and covered with textile or leather. They often had front legs of a kind first seen in some Queen Anne chairs and known as 'cabriole legs'. Besides having great style, the broad 'knee' with its large jointing surfaces made it possible to leave out the stiffening rails between the legs.

The breadth of the seat and the backward-swept arm-supports remind us that clothes were so wide, stiff and bunchy that the chair had to provide for their sweeping out at the sides.

The first wave of foreign influence in the eighteenth century was, as to interior design, formal and chilly. It was followed not unnaturally by a light, pretty style, featuring tiny repetitive ornament, pastel colours and gilt. Chairs followed suit, and the great names surviving from this time are those of the Adam Brothers, interior architects, and Hepplewhite and Sheraton, furniture designers. The craftsmen took advantage of the use of small motifs such as ears of wheat devised by the Adams. Furniture was often painted, not with a few slaps of the brush but with a satiny pastel groundwork on which were put, with a fine brush, delicate flowers and flower-like designs, even tiny landscapes with figures. Besides all this, chairs could have textile backs and seats, often in satin. Hepplewhite and his followers preferred carved and polished wood, and devised pretty chair backs, sometimes almost heart-shaped, and decorated with swags, wheatsheaves and ears of corn. Such chairs were intended to blend with the rooms whose details were attended to by the Adams: the mirrors, picture frames, overmantels, door furniture, candle sconces, everything.

All this time of course we have been thinking of the homes and possessions of the rich and powerful. What the working people had was considered of little account, a mere fumbling with simple tools and cheap materials.

Nevertheless a world-famous type of chair emerged from the woods of Berkshire in England, where small workshops were sited among the trees. These 'Windsor' chairs employed several fascinating techniques; first, spindle-turning. This is done on a lathe and for a chair the object is to make thin tapering pieces of wood which, when set fan-wise into the chairback, give spring when the sitter leans back. These chairs, with and without arms, are still made. The seats are of solid wood hollowed to fit the sitter; it is said that the original pattern was made in soft clay. When everything is rightly made and angled these chairs can be more comfortable than padded chairs designed mainly for their looks.

*'Windsor' chair*

*Victorian deep-buttoned chair*

We are still nowhere near the time when ordinary people expected to be able comfortably to loll in a chair. This only came about in roughly the lifetime of the oldest person alive today. Until the late nineteenth century neither men nor women dressed so that they could relax in a chair. It is almost impossible to imagine the unrelaxed sitting habits of our great-grandparents.

But again, the taste of women seems to have asserted itself. Among a hotch-potch of unattractive and uncomfortable nineteenth-century chairs, one kind stands out. It was low, deeply upholstered and deep-buttoned, a real woman's chair and now eagerly sought after in antique shops and re-upholstered with loving care. It is certainly the forerunner of some of our cosy upholstered plywood and fibreglass chairs of today.

The nineteenth century was an age of factory experiment, patchy, unguided, insensitive, chaotic. But nevertheless one can 'spot' Victorian objects, including chairs, as easily as those of the eighteenth century when the whole business of consistent design was a governing idea.

*'Club' chair*

But the twentieth century—the lifetime of people only now in their sixties! What chairs they have had! What softness and depth! What shaping to the body! What care that the sitter's weight shall be evenly distributed over surfaces curved and softened to receive it! And the new materials that designers can play with, even for factory production—ply-woods, metal, fibreglass, rubber, even cardboard and paper, softened with plastic foam and covered over with stretch or ordinary textiles.

It has at last been realised that function has a priority with chairs. All this vigorous development can be laid at the door of modern, well-trained designers working in industry for progressive firms. The 'pace of modern life' has brought its reward, luxurious chairs to relax in, available to almost anyone who wants one.

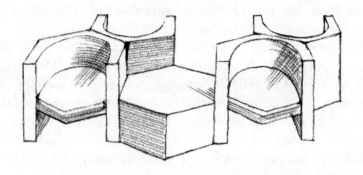

This short survey of the development of chairs could be matched by a study of tables, cupboards, chests-of-drawers, all the standard pieces of furniture that despite fashion have been needed by people down the centuries. One could follow and examine in the same way other common possessions such as eating implements, home lighting, cooking ware and so on.

We would find the same uncertain balance between function and appearance, like the strict functional bias of the Windsor chair as against the strict fashionableness of Sheraton. And with the changes in fashion there was either more or less feeling for durability. The more emphatic the fashion content, the less the emphasis on long life.

All designing is like this. At the moment the civilised world is emerging from a period of great feeling for function into a time of great delight in decorative quality.

But here is a problem. Can a machine decorate? If so, how? If our lives are surrounded by quantities of decoration all alike, how can it fail to become boring?

Of course endless repetition of decorative elements does become boring. It is a contradiction in terms. Decoration arose as a form of relief to the eye, which likes variety. We have here a built-in incentive to speed up change so that nothing stays with us long enough to bore us. The equivalent of paper dresses has not yet reached the ordinary home furnishings, but one must be wary in furnishing of a repetitive and meaningless design language like a gramophone record with the needle stuck in a groove, of design clichés in fact. Furnishings are not cheap to change.

We have looked at Design from various points of view—the critic's, the shopper's, the user's, the designer's and the historian's.

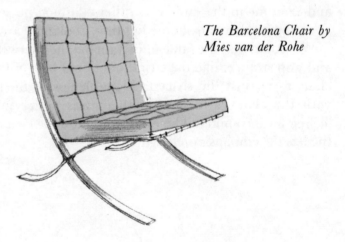

*The Barcelona Chair by Mies van der Rohe*

The shopper and the user, not always the same person, are non-specialised. But a knowledge of design can affect the comfort, convenience and the pocket of both.

The designer and the critic are specialists. They are both interesting people to know, workers for the good of others, responsible to the public for what they do and say, the mentors of the manufacturers and retailers, public authorities and building firms, all of whom might overlook the consumer amid all their other preoccupations.

The design historian studies an aspect of society. His study brings in peoples' customs, habits, clothes, tastes, incomes, social standing, the whole weaving pageant of human society down the ages.

This is a vast subject, rightly seen. One could try studying a small part—lamp-posts or fireguards or fire engines or locks and hinges, or curtainings.

It will be found that one is really investigating the lives of people, investigating people themselves. Design is one of the ways in which people and societies write their own history for those who know how to read it.

Design is a language. It is talking all the time. Try to understand what it is saying.

# INDEX